3am Songbook

3am Songbook

A Collection of Poems
to Uplift Your Heart

Brian Joseph Jeffries

This book is dedicated to my amazing wife for all of her love and support throughout our entire life together. We've been on many adventures and have many more to come. Above all, I dedicate this book to God for saving my life.

Contents

Acknowledgments

I have so many people to thank, I've decided to express my gratitude in a poem. My "Thank You Song" is a lyrical poem written for all of the many people who have helped and influenced me over the years which inspired me to write this collection.

Psalms 95:2 (ESV)
"Let us come into his presence with thanksgiving; let us make a joyful noise to him with songs of praise!"

Introduction

I started waking up at 3am and began writing down my thoughts and dreams. I was on a journey with the Lord and was filling my notebook with songs of my life. Eventually, I was writing throughout the days and nights, a combination of new things along with my life's experiences. I felt as if I was writing words that were given to me through divine inspiration, but this did not happen until God woke me up to life.

These poems are about the battles of good and evil, with the focus on God and positivity. They are told in a variety of ways focusing on family, friends, pets, careers, countless musicians, writers, entertainers, youtuber's, movies, etc. that have played an inspirational role in my life. Anything that was once negative has now been turned positive.

I began my career in the electrical trade. My childhood friend Brian introduced me to firefighting. I joined a volunteer fire company in Seaville, NJ and enjoyed being a firefighter. I then went to school to become an EMT and joined the local rescue squad in Upper Township, NJ. Everyone was very supportive at both places and had a huge impact on helping guide me on my path. I felt the medical career was for me, so I continued on to paramedic school and eventually became a flight paramedic. I was also teaching EMT and paramedic classes along with AHA courses.

I felt it was a gift to be able to help people in all different situations. I definitely learned a lot about life while running the streets and flying the skies as a paramedic. I was able to work with and meet many great people in the field and was always learning new things. Although at times it was a difficult and challenging career, I enjoyed being a paramedic. I've wanted to help people my entire life. I was definitely blessed in this career, but something didn't feel right. It had been an amazing journey, but I felt there was something more.

After being in a car accident in 2011, I found out I had cervical disc injuries and a cyst in my spinal cord. I had permanent nerve damage and lost sensation in my left arm from the elbow down, which ended my flight paramedic career. Eventually I regained strength in my arm and got back into the field and started teaching too. Every year I had to get an MRI to monitor the cyst for growth. In the spring of 2018, my MRI revealed something new. As stated by my doctor, "it's a miracle, the cyst in your spinal cord has disappeared." It's amazing how many miracles happen every day.

After years of working in EMS, I was unable to hide my emotions anymore. The nightmares in my mind were becoming overwhelming. I was struggling to maintain my career as a paramedic. Even after going from the streets to teaching, it didn't matter. I had dealt with anxiety and depression my entire life and in the recent years added PTSD to the list.

The darkness had finally consumed me, and I hit rock bottom. It was at that time I called out to Jesus like never before, then things began to change. My depression and anxiety now became visions of an amazing world I did not know existed. Jesus had definitely answered my call.

I believed in God, but always had a lot of questions. I hadn't gone to church for many years. I realized I knew of God but did not really know Him. I turned to the Bible and realized that to get my head right, I needed to get my heart right. I started studying the Bible and going to church again.

Music, pets, motorcycles and nature have been therapeutic for me since I was a child. Now I've added writing too. I feel we all have our own version of a book to write. I would urge anyone struggling with anything in life to reach out to God and see that the negative world they may be living in, does not have to stay that way. He will show you the way. As a work in progress, I'm learning how to address any difficulties or frustrations more appropriately now. Struggles will come, but through faith, I'm more prepared to respond to them. I feel as anyone in sports has told us, when you lose a game, put it behind you and prepare for the next one.

Follow your dreams, don't settle for: "I can't" or "that's just the way it's always been." Make a change in your life and see how God will show you things that you never thought were possible. That's what I've done, and I'm excited to start this new calling and adventure as a writer and lyricist. I pray this book of life's journey blesses you all.

Now, I invite you on a journey, through the depths of your mind's movie screen, to the rainbow's end, along a golden road of eternity. The time is now to come together, all the people of every nation, across this universe of a life without boundaries.

I got an early morning wake-up call from God about our lives that have true meaning, for which you're permanently awake and you never stop dreaming. There are limitless possibilities through a symphony message of hope and rhythmic positivity. Let's take a voyage in this supernatural world, beyond the realm of a comfortable existence of routine.

We're living in the now, of a life less ordinary, on an angelic adventure of faith in God's amazing story. Winning a galactic battle of good and evil, His light shines down upon us, forever in His glory. We see a reflection into a world of peace, through the eyes of our hearts. Unity is the message, for which we all can begin to start. Through the lyrics of our life's dream, I welcome you to my heart and soul. Let's begin and I'll show you what I mean.

Theater of Dreams

From a dream I awoke
In my notebook I wrote
"Listen to the words they're in you,
This is what your life is going to be,
Writing down the words, for all the world to see"

God wakes us up, sometimes around three
He's got so much to say, to you and to me
I've opened my spiritual, eyes and ears
While in the darkest of night, I have no fears
The eyes of my heart, are now enlightened
Dark side of my mind, has been brightened

Take a ride, in that mystery machine
His love will open you, to the world unseen
Remember MLK Jr, he had a dream
The world was intended, to be one team
We're all one in God's nation, upon this earth
Helping to start, this immense rebirth
When you awake and realize, we're not all machines
Turn on your heart, to God's theater of dreams

Heard the voice of God, in those early morning hours
Through the Lord, He gives us power
The lyrics to me, He has given
A gift from God, in this vessel I'm driven
To spread His word, on the wings of a dove
Freedom's ringing in our ears, song notes of peace and love
Giving me messages, all through the night
Now that I know, how to listen to 'em right

Sometimes you'll awake, with a new kinda knowing
Jesus is knocking, His love He is showing
Went the distance, found the sunlight at night
I'm back on my feet, He's brightened my sight

The glare and the beam, what was happening to me
Loving this life, a new peace decree
Now's the time, let's all come together
We're a world of one, and Christ is the tether

Take a ride, in that mystery machine
His love will open you, to the world unseen
Remember MLK Jr, he had a dream
The world was intended, to be one team
We're all one in God's nation, upon this earth
Helping to start, this immense rebirth
When you awake and realize, we're not all machines
Turn on your heart, to God's theater of dreams

Joel 2:28 (ESV)

"And it shall come to pass afterward, that I will pour out my Spirit on all flesh; your sons and your daughters shall prophesy, your old men shall dream dreams, and your young men shall see visions."

My Dear Friend Vincent

Seeing is believing, may not always be so
The air around us, hiding more than you know
Believing is seeing
Within all human beings
Starry night painting, more accurately displays
Flow of earth's energy, around us everyday

Vincent like many, troubled and depressed
Struggled with demons, in life's stress test
No one would listen, to the messages he had
If they'd opened their minds, they would have been glad

My dear friend Vincent
Your mind may have been distant
You had a gift from the Lord
Seems hard to understand, what you were heading toward
Found the missing peace, to the puzzles that we paint
We're listening now, this time we will not faint

With a new brush, Vincent's loving hand is back
Another starry night, is painted 'cross the black
Always get back up, whenever you fall
We're all painters on God's canvas, in His glory we stand in awe

There are monsters in this world, that lurk in the unseen
Not everyone can see them, through their hidden smokescreens
He had abundant gifts, but constant battles with the beast
Pushed him to the breaking point, the fear became increased
Started a new painting, turning evol back to love
Endless color options, from the palette up above

The time has come
For the battle's already been won
Although difficult and tiresome
Evil has been overcome
Soon people will realize
So much of the world's real lies

14

With a new brush, Vincent's loving hand is back
Another starry night, is painted 'cross the black
Always get back up, whenever you fall
We're all painters on God's canvas, in His glory we stand in awe

Can't always believe what you see
It's all become so clear to me
I know that believing is seeing
Some may ask, what do you mean
God has given us a gift
Deception's curtain, we'll all lift

I now understand, how Don McLean
Painted a portrait, of Vincent's life and pain
Other people's madness
Can turn into your sadness
Years gone by, they didn't know how
Seems that they all, are listening now

Wheat field thunder cloud, eternity's gate
Gone too soon, for fate would not wait
In these days, keep saying your prayers
Soon we'll be headin', up those heavenly stairs
Vincent's now peaceful, for this I know
Live your life now, paint your own Van Gogh

Antenna of Love

Pool cue's clearing the table
Love is back ready, willing and able
The heart of a locket
Sending peace to every pocket
Tune your heart's radio, to human being
As you can see, the evil is fleeing
Gotta love one another, my sisters and brothers
Now is the time, unlike any other

The destructive signal, has been shut down
It's God's peace that's now, going out to every town
For too long, love's signal they've been jammin'
No need to get back, to your regularly scheduled programmin'
From Wardenclyffe in New York, to the Paris Eiffel Tower
Love's going 'round the world, you can feel God's power

Antenna of love
The peace of a dove
We're talkin' worldwide K-Love
Spreading love on every station
Sending peace and love to every nation
Making sense of this abomination

Father's peace and love
Eternal from above
Rewrite our history
Sailing God's frequent sea
His plan has come
For us all to be one

The deception has been lifted
God's people have been gifted
As the new generations
He'll save all the nations

Set the volume to max
Love will stop the attacks
In this life some call a game
Remember Thy name

Antenna of love
The peace of a dove
We're talkin' worldwide K-Love
Spreading love on every station
Sending peace and love to every nation
Making sense of this abomination

We're all Scooby Doo
The mystery's in you
There's work to be done
Remember through all we are one
A world of paradise is to come
Welcome back to God's kingdom

1 John 4:7 (ESV)

"Beloved, let us love one another, for love is from God, and whoever loves has been born of God and knows God."

My Wife

Just as the Dude, I'll always abide
Happily married, and enjoying the ride
Her swirl of cocoa galaxy eyes
Brighten the darkest of any skies
Promise 'til the end of time
A Pink Floyd nursery rhyme
Hand in hand, and heart to heart
Together forever, never be apart

My heart can't stop smiling
Since the day you wore my ring
Bodyguard has us covered, underneath His wing
I'll be your Costner, you'll be my Whitney
Livin' together, in this world of Disney

In this new year, our love it shines
Like God's music notes, so divine
Got across that river, to be with my wife
Lord knows she's so fine, she brings such beauty to life
Celebrated 25 married years in the making
Always try to live, with more giving than taking

As the sun rises, a beautiful red dawn
We are birds in this painting, that He has drawn
God's morning skywriter
Paints with a purple rain highlighter
Love you pumpkin, my favorite pie
You've saved my life, that ain't no lie

My heart can't stop smiling
Since the day you wore my ring
Bodyguard has us covered, underneath His wing
I'll be your Costner, you'll be my Whitney
Livin' together, in this world of Disney

From those Firehouse days as a trainee
To where my heart is now set free
You've always been there for me
Together we're stronger, a love guarantee
I've never had to wonder
I'll always be your thunder
Lady, you look wonderful tonight
His plan made our hearts, as one unite

This love of a lifetime,
was sent from above
We just couldn't help,
falling in love
How beautiful my darling,
sunshine rose among the thorns
Through the challenges before us,
we've weathered every storm
Blessed are those,
that are thankful for this life
Moral of the story,
I'm thankful for my wife

Proverbs 18:22 (ESV)

*"He who finds a wife finds a good thing
and obtains favor from the Lord."*

Renovate Your Heart

The highest of price, has already been paid
What sometimes may seem, to be poorly made
Is actually the builder's, design incentives
Strengthening our heart, for future endeavors
Constructing the framework, of Holy Spirit relations
His peace will take, away our frustrations
Reclaim your heart, like vintage hardwood floors
And use that old wood, for a beautiful new door

Magnolia company, the town or the tree
Pastor Bill, Milestone Church, helped set me free
Work's always in progress, don't build your castle on sand
Jesus is the rock, strongest in the land
Don't hang a picture, to hide your heart's cracked wall
In this real estate of life, be an investor when God calls

God renovates your heart
Even before you decide to start
King of King's builders, starring Chip and Jo
Offers a home warranty, giving the confidence you know
A strong foundation stands firm, passed the test
Transform your heart like those homes, with the Savior's best
When construction of life, becomes too heavy
Pray, take a deep breath, and carry the "e"

Early morning writing lyrics, 2 and 3 am
That rewind button, is now working again
New power source, in our universal remote control
Love's clear coat of protection, on our heart and soul
We're doin' it right, this time around
Stopped the demolition crew's, evil countdown

God renovates your heart
Even before you decide to start
King of King's builders, starring Chip and Jo
Offers a home warranty, giving the confidence you know
A strong foundation stands firm, passed the test
Transform your heart like those homes, with the Savior's best
When construction of life, becomes too heavy
Pray, take a deep breath, and carry the "e"

Romans 8:28 (KJV)

"And we know that all things work together for good to them that love God, to them who are called according to his purpose."

www.milestonenj.org

Jesus Got Our Six

My friend Don and I
Just had a slice, of American Pie
Down at the corner cafe
Is where we met one day
We talked about, what the people might say
When they see God's always winning, and is here to stay

Train's back from the coast
From the highest of most
Church bells again are ringing
My three best friends, you'll hear 'em singing
Creating light from sound
The answer has been found
Won the war of the spirits, on earth's battleground

Jesus got our six
As we stand holding hands, at our nine and three
Together we are friends, one family
Jesus got our six
We will honor Thee
Standing tall, for all the world to see

At a local bar, in a town called earth
That's where we'll witness, this world's rebirth
At life's crossroads, feelin' overjoyed
That old contract's, now null 'n void
No more evil, no more strife
Dull is both sides, the devil's knife

As we walked off the stage
A band of many age
My man Charlie said, with a smirk in his gaze
Last time I'm tellin' ya son of a gun
We're the best of all these days

Jesus got our six
As we stand holding hands, at our nine and three
Together we are friends, one family
Jesus got our six
We will honor Thee
Standing tall, for all the world to see

As we drew a toke
He stood there, in the fog of smoke
For Satan's spell, yes it had been broke
All he could do, is look down at his feet
For he knew, this had been his defeat
Jesus has, defibbed our hearts
The music's back, time for a new start

This generation's, no longer lost in space
Music and faith, setting free the human race
Angels are singing, to make us all smile
Levee's no longer dry, we've opened the Nile

Jesus got our six
As we stand holding hands, at our nine and three
Together we are friends, one family
Jesus got our six
We will honor Thee
Standing tall, for all the world to see

It's now everyone's chance
Let's all get up and dance
Put on your footloose dancin' shoes
Cause we're no longer, singin' the blues
The sacred store, now's got some happy news

Colossians 3:16 (KJV)

"Let the word of Christ dwell in you richly in all wisdom; teaching and admonishing one another in psalms and hymns and spiritual songs, singing with grace in your hearts to the Lord."

Pet by Your Side

Here's a little story, 'bout a man and his dog
She's the therapy, when my mind's in a fog
Cute yellow lab, whose love is sublime
Everyone loves her, her name is Sunshine

The Word of God, has been speakin' to my heart
Feel my life's second act, is about to start
Went out walking, with a bible and my Sunny
We had a little talk, bet it looked kinda funny
Said feel like I'm ready, to begin livin' this dream
Feelin' strong and prepared, to join the team

My dog turned to me, these words she said
Tennessee or New York, the place we should head
Or go down to Florida, and relax instead
I said are you Sirius, is it time to go
I'm your rainbow dog star, you already know

Fill your water bowl with love, let the Son shine in
Live like our pets, their heart's pure from within
Rise above the stress, and enjoy life's ride
Hold your head high, with your pet by your side

Anything's possible, don't stop believin'
Threw out that ball and she went retrievin'
Even when you fake it, they run after that toy
They trust that you threw it, playing is what they enjoy

We can all feel better, with good belly rubs
Cross paw peace, enjoying kisses and hugs
Purrin' like a Hemi, the coolest of cats
Together they play, two kids being brats

Times can be rough, from Rocky to Smooth
Look to the heavens, ask what's my next move
When life catches you strugglin', with your pants down
Pull 'em up tight, wrap Orion's belt around
Catching frosty snowballs, while playing in life's backyard
Simple and yet so fun, helps when the days are hard

Fill your water bowl with love, let the Son shine in
Live like our pets, their heart's pure from within
Rise above the stress, and enjoy life's ride
Hold your head high, with your pet by your side

We drive around town, face in the wind
Nothin' bringin' us down, every day's the weekend
Always happy to see us, with excitement so kind
They love at all times, no matter what troubles our mind
Top down and cruisin', a Jeep wave we're giving
Radio pumpin', our favorite songs we're singing

Curled up together, the couch where we Schnug
Fill up with love, the hole that life's dug
Happy today, regardless of money
A walk in the park, nature, bees and Honey
With God and your family, life's full of joy
Like when the bark box comes, with your doggie's new toy

Fill your water bowl with love, let the Son shine in
Live like our pets, their heart's pure from within
Rise above the stress, and enjoy life's ride
Hold your head high, with your pet by your side

For our pets that have passed, and are no longer with us
I've seen them in Sunshine, have faith and trust
They're forever around us, I have no doubt
In a heavenly park, they are playing about
Furry family love, that turns our nightmares to Christmas
We're like Jack or Sally, with our Zero flying with us

They helped get us through life, the joy and the pain
Although we don't see them, I feel they remain
Now crossed, that rainbow bridge of a star
They're playing the strings, of our heart's guitar

As this story comes to a close, again went out for a drive
They're always happy with us, just being alive
Racing thoughts in my mind, then began to calm
Feeling stronger now, thinking 91st Psalm

Pondered and realized, the pet by my side
Seems like the one, taking me for the ride
Wash your soul's water bowl, don't let it dry, refill it
Got a dream with a plan, time to start, go fulfill it

Armor of God

Put on the armor of God, be protected by the belt of truth
God's righteousness is for us all, no need to change in a phone booth
Helmet of salvation, gives us confidence to go forward
If lost in a sea of despair, His love will lead you shoreward

While sailing the universal waters, keep God as your rudder
May your heart flow from life's wellspring, with the words you utter
God's servants of New Jerusalem, in a circle gathered 'round
Ripple in the wind, hear the voice of a unified sound

Shoes of peace cover our feet, and help to share good news
Standing up to any challenge, with Him we'll never lose
On par with the beat drummin' in my soul, my heart's an open book
Your questions can be answered, give the Bible a look

While sailing the universal waters, keep God as your rudder
May your heart flow from life's wellspring, with the words you utter
God's servants of New Jerusalem, in a circle gathered 'round
Ripple in the wind, hear the voice of a unified sound

A shield of faith stops the arrows, that come from every angle
God's Word is ammunition, to stand against satan's lies entangled
Truth and wisdom of our home, God has been revealing
Raining His Word through the masses, from this leaking ceiling

While sailing the universal waters, keep God as your rudder
May your heart flow from life's wellspring, with the words you utter
God's servants of New Jerusalem, in a circle gathered 'round
Ripple in the wind, hear the voice of a unified sound

Ephesians 6:11 (ESV)
"Put on the whole armor of God, that you may be able to stand against the schemes of the devil."

29

Two-Wheeled Therapy

On a horse of steel, these streets I ride
Evil's tryin' to get me, but I'm still alive
Learn to feel the power
While seizing the hour
Now awake I've realized, to go live the dream
It's motorcycle music, when those pipes scream

While riding through Sewell
Saw a church sign so cool
It said, "Exercise daily, run from the devil
Walk with God", in His glory we'll revel
Detroit's Kid Rock, I love you man
Means so much, for which you stand
Singin' born free with faith, on an open road
Pull the throttle back, let the mind unload
On a pair of wheels we travel, along life's highway
A tour of freedom, God Bless the USA

Four way stop, at life's crossroads of wild
Been riding the wind, since I was a child
His helmet of salvation, protects me on the road
He's the headlight of the world, our computer's source code
Jesus in my sidecar, brought my heart such clarity
Take a little time, for some two-wheeled therapy

Jammin' tunes through the hills, heart's no longer dead
Enjoy the sunshine daydream, flowing through your head
Feeling grateful with Jerry, and the rest of the band
Sunlight shines upon us, all over this land
Me and my girl, on the Harley cruisin'
Through scarlet begonias, ain't no way we're losin'

Hangin' out with LL Cool J and Run DMC
Can't live without my radio, turn up the rock box with me
A weekend in New England, in a Manilow mood
Landscape of a painting, hungry for some food
Been riding through, those honeysuckle breezes
Stopped at the vineyard, for some wine and cheeses
Any make or model, they're all the same to Jesus

Four way stop, at life's crossroads of wild
Been riding the wind, since I was a child
His helmet of salvation, protects me on the road
He's the headlight of the world, our computer's source code
Jesus in my sidecar, brought my heart such clarity
Take a little time, for some two-wheeled therapy

Nikola Tesla

Man with a plan, the greater good of the earth
Time has arrived, for the great rebirth
Aurora Borealis, been given me a feeling
There's a hole in this, Truman Show's glass ceiling
No need for oil, with a Tesla coil
Heat from deception's, brought this world to a boil

A triangle key, to the world we know
Healing us all, the capstone's now aglow
We're gonna play, that secret chord
You know the one, that pleased the Lord
God's alarm clock is ringing
A love song from Tesla we're singing

"Your kingdom come, Your will be done,
On earth as it is in heaven"
Jesus' returning soon, the hour's eleven
A circle of life, earth is the name tag
Large yet small, like marbles in a bag
Seems the sounds that we hear
Can be seen crystal clear

Free people and energy, free the world for all
God's children are awake, we've answered the call
We're the ones, to make a brighter day
Lovelight is on, just follow His way
Cue the peace to the puzzle, the love, the Son
Energy's all around us, time to free everyone

Tune up and activate, the pyramid's power
Perfect harmony and understanding, in this golden hour
Spreading God's love, in a 432 vibrational shower
Pie in the sky, a divine Wardenclyffe tower
In an awakening world, that is magnetic
Choose to create love, that is energetic

We now know the frequencies Kenneth
Battle's been won, with the seal of the seventh
Chess match of life against death, it's not too late
The knight has put the grim reaper, into checkmate
God's love's going out, to every town
Time to put on, your wedding gown

Tesla's the man, who's been kept out of our history
Suppressing his knowledge, only making a mystery
His contributions to humanity, so many used everyday
His greater plan we'll bring to life, for there is a better way
Human radio has set, love's signal to repeat
We knew all along, that God can't be beat

Free people and energy, free the world for all
God's children are awake, we've answered the call
We're the ones, to make a brighter day
Lovelight is on, just follow His way
Cue the peace to the puzzle, the love, the Son
Energy's all around us, time to free everyone

Evil signal's been shut down, we can all take a breath
No need to be afraid, of the illusion of death
With the Son, everything is in tune
From earth, to the bright side of the moon
Tomorrowland is happening, no need to ask how
Soon the world will see, the truth that is now

Let's live the movie, Tesla a Life Unedited
We'll play supporting roles, as angels of power unlimited
We're all learning more facts, of our true history
An adjustment to the ending, a new beginning victory
Supernatural film of truth, on this world's silver screen
A documentary beyond, what you've ever seen

Mark 9:23 (ESV)
"...all things are possible for one who believes."

A New Old Psalm

Look up, take courage, get your heart nsync
God's angels are nearer, than you might think
After all these years, they're all together
Helping rid us of fears, you may hear their feathers
Pay attention world, for this is God's plan
He loves us all, every woman and man

Sands of time were running low, but now we're able
To spin the hourglass, that was stuck to the table
We are the generation, that knows how
No need to fear, we're in God's hands now
Like my twisted sister said, we're not gonna take it
We'll take our stand, together we'll make it

No matter how, stormy the weathers
God will cover you, with His feathers
Under His wings, you will find refuge
Like Noah had, during the deluge
His faithfulness will be, your shield and rampart
For God's love, will transform your heart

Signal's been sent, will you answer the call
No more SOS in distress, now peace and love for all
The skillet is hot, with a bright loving flame
Rise and revolution, we're changing the game
Eyes of the Lord, over the righteous and lost
He already paid the price, for us there is no cost

His ears are open, unto our prayers
Look for that ladder, climb those golden stairs
As the horn sounds, Michael will stand up
Now is the time, to fill your cup
You just need to ask, He'll overflow His
Trust in your gut, while taking life's quiz

No matter how, stormy the weathers
God will cover you, with His feathers
Under His wings, you will find refuge
Like Noah had, during the deluge
His faithfulness will be, your shield and rampart
For God's love, will transform your heart

He has given, His angels charge
The wicked can't survive, in a love so large
Arrows now seem dull, with no sharpener available
There's no mountain task, that is not scalable
Ten thousand may, fall around me
There no evil, shall befall thee
Angel's been uniting, breaking the chains
Steering stars a new direction, with God at the reigns

Psalms 91:2,4 (KJV)

"I will say of the Lord, He is my refuge and my fortress: my God; in him will I trust. He shall cover thee with his feathers, and under his wings shalt thou trust: his truth shall be thy shield..."

Peace on My Side

The peace on my side, a Psalm 91
It's different than, your average gun
If you are peaceful, or on the run
Psalm 91, can't be outdone
Peace for any age, teach your children young
About life, the Bible, and your Psalm 91

Those arrows that, fly by everyday
Don't seem to trouble me, like yesterday
I'll always be strong, no matter what the haters say
He gives me courage, while living this dream
Will not back down, love is the theme

While traveling through, this great land
A simple hello, or shake of the hand
A hopeful smile, can go a long way
Doesn't matter if, you don't know what to say
Just listening can, brighten someone's day
While on this trip, follow your tour guide
I'll always have Jesus, the peace on my side

He's commanded his angels, to guard over our ways
An inspirational ballet, of these glorious new days
Jesus keeps leading us, as we go
After all He's the one, running this show
Happiness and joy, is what we feel
Peace in our hearts, His love is real

When we make it to, the Promised Land
I'll still carry, my peace in my hand
Singin' the love, no matter the band
My holster carries, God's music my friend
I'll be armed with His love, until the end

While traveling through, this great land
A simple hello, or shake of the hand
A hopeful smile, can go a long way
Doesn't matter if, you don't know what to say
Just listening can, brighten someone's day
While on this trip, follow your tour guide
I'll always have Jesus, the peace on my side

The Return

Question for us to ponder, what if real is the dream
There are many of you out there, that know what I mean
Pay attention in this life, things aren't always as they seem
Look for the meaning, like in this song of many themes
What's real or fantasy, open your mind and you'll see
Your heart is the key, love will set you free

No such thing as coincidence, things happen for a reason
Many signals from the Lord,
to get us through the toughest seasons
Inspirational messages of God, Shelley does preach
We're all starting to live, a Charlie Chaplin speech

God's here to stay
Each and every day
Tell your story to all
God has made the call
No more living in fear
Jesus' return is near

No longer a lost boy, but still forever Peter Pan
On timeless journeys, to the islands of Neverland
Been taking my time, writing with a slow hand
Holy Spirit's awakened me, to join the band
Eyes wide open, heading to the Holy Land

Some run the hamster wheel, floating in the sky
Others in the cage, as their life passes by
We can all break free, you just gotta try
Time for this evil world, to say goodbye
We're makin' a move, beginning to set things right
Time to put on, a Johnny Cash suit of white

God's here to stay
Each and every day
Tell your story to all
God has made the call
No more living in fear
Jesus' return is near

Unplug from, the matrix of deception
Wake up and receive, there's no exception
Just do the math, you'll find your path
It's a new day, God will show you the way
Bible Project crew, get your learn on with the Lord
A priceless education, that anyone can afford

Lessons from Dorothy, helped this tin man find his heart
Showed me the brains and courage, had been there from the start
We have Glenda's in our lives, kind and loving while called witches
It's the evil ones, that digs our mind of shallow ditches
We've sailed beyond, the road of yellow brick
Still standing through it all, brought Oz that old broomstick

Through journeys on this path unknown, we're never on our own
Call God the great and powerful one, there's no place like His home
Tell everyone from east to west, through all the atmosphere
It appears very clear, the return of Jesus is near

Matthew 24:36 (ESV)

"But concerning that day and hour no one knows, not even the angels of heaven, nor the Son, but the Father only."

Amanda's Field

Squad 21 and Station 19
New beginnings for me, while still quite green
Although nervous and scared
One thing's for sure, I knew that I cared
Coming home that day, with a force from behind
Seems your role, had already been assigned
Heaven's now home, we'll see you in time
Forever in your family's heart and in mine

While at Amanda's Field, or at the skatepark
Let the light in, whenever it's dark
Throughout the year, and every 4th of July
When you sit in the field, and look to the sky
Her goodness shines through, for everyone to see
Over the field by her home, in South Jersey

Her light disappeared, or so it may seem
She'll shine on forever, in this life but a dream
Sometimes things happen, can't dwell on the fault
Don't let those demons, build up in your vault
Many have nightmares, that get really bad
Think of the good things, it helps with the sad

While at Amanda's Field, or at the skatepark
Let the light in, whenever it's dark
Throughout the year, and every 4th of July
When you sit in the field, and look to the sky
Her goodness shines through, for everyone to see
Over the field by her home, in South Jersey

The past is behind us, can only forgive
No matter what happens, we all gotta live
While brightest of spirits, within this life
Now your light's blinding, in this world's afterlife
No longer here, it's hard to conceive
Our souls carry on, you just gotta believe

While at Amanda's Field, or at the skatepark
Let the light in, whenever it's dark
Throughout the year, and every 4th of July
When you sit in the field, and look to the sky
Her goodness shines through, for everyone to see
Over the field by her home, in South Jersey

On the side of that road, along with your family
Your soul had passed on, I felt you around me
There are angels everywhere, no need to ask why
From friends to a stranger, not just up in the sky
Everyone's an angel - you, thee, and I
Although not here in body, her spirit's alive
Shining bright forever, over Sunset Drive

Matthew 5:16 (ESV)
*"In the same way, let your light shine before others, so that they may see your
good works and give glory to your Father who is in heaven."*

Floydian Slip

Hi guys, wait 'til ya see
Something special, for you from me
A song for all, the Pink Floyd family
Not able to ease, my mind of fears
Your sounds in my ears, helped stop the tears
Didn't realize my current self, had already died
Couldn't do it on my own, although I had tried
Playing medicine for the soul, that's what I do
Enjoy nature's beauty, and listen to you

Polly writing with David, pick up this heaven's brochure
Let's all come together, for this Floyd grand tour
England's Amazing David Gilmour Best Ever
Mnemonic for guitar strings, thought it kinda clever
Listening to the songs of David, calms the mind
A Pink Floyd prescription, there's no better kind
They're not FDA approved, but man can they groove
Take as needed, your heart light will improve

A smile that's Rich with light
Sometimes it just feels Wright
Volume's pumping, we're feeling overjoyed
On a journey of hope, while listening to some Floyd
Shining bright beyond the end
That verse is for you my friend

Finally stopped, I had been runnin' away
Stood against evil, now I've got somethin' to say
After many years, been splashed by the Holy water gun
Now awake and on the go, life's for livin' and for fun
Gonna shine among them, sparkling stars in the sky
No more fear and anxiety, not afraid to die

This shining soul's no longer lost, down the rabbit hole
We're taking it back now, that fiddle the devil stole
Coming back to life, hear cries of freedom from our horns
Clearing our hearts field, full of barbed wire thorns
Roger got us through, when those waters were rough
Fight the good fight, no matter how tough
World leaders unite, and bring us all together
Spread our wings of peace, as one primary feather

Pink has said it for years
Please open up your ears
In this wind of change, we've found our rhyme
Awakened today, just in the Nick of time
Thank You Syd, for sharing your dreams
Maybe that's, what his name means
Geldof and Parker, showed us an amazing wall
Had been there with an arctic heart, until I got the call

Alice's tea set with the madcap laughs, rise above all
Made it past the Atari game, of life's pitfalls
It's a miracle this life, and we ain't seen nothin' yet
It all makes perfect sense, soon we'll see it in the gazette
The time has come, to play our worldwide anthem
Dawning of a new age, who could have ever fathomed
This dream is now an orchestra, playing a symphony of love
We've heard the tolling of the bell, thank you to the Lord above

Finally stopped, I had been runnin' away
Stood against evil, now I've got somethin' to say
After many years, been splashed by the Holy water gun
Now awake and on the go, life's for livin' and for fun
Gonna shine among them, sparkling stars in the sky
No more fear and anxiety, not afraid to die

We can all learn to fly, in time the truth we'll unveil
The soldier made it back, to narrate a happy tale
We've battled many demons, finally figured it out
Sharing the good news, we'll stand up and shout
Their sounds resonate, to take you higher
Ignites the spark, in your soul's amplifier
Does anybody know, which one is Pink
Peer into the mirror, least that's what I think

Storm of art, on every album cover
Just my little song, for any Pink Floyd lover
Every person plays a part, take any one away
It wouldn't be Pink Floyd, the way we know them today
Thank you for this music, helps us keep a balance on this trip
Set your heart's compass to onward, on your Floydian ship
Question to us all, is this just a Floydian slip

Heartlight Hotel

My heart light went, from red to green
Finally on the go, you know what I mean
Spoke with God, and Elvis in a dream
About our life's, eternal balance beam

Sail away, on this sea of love
When the waters get rough, He'll lift us on wings of a dove
Misery and fear, to them we're saying farewell
Jesus shut down, the Heartbreak Hotel

The twisted heart's knot, He's been untying
As it grows large, you begin to stop crying
Keep hope alive, while dodging those spears
Use your key of life, to lock out the fears

The road was rough, we went through hell
We've now opened, the Heartlight Hotel
Joyful stories of life, is what we'll tell
Glory to God, we will yell
A green light special, on aisle five
A once dark heart, now full of love and alive

The clerk's tears, are no longer flowing
Bellhop's now dressed in white, God's love I am knowing
At the Heartlight Hotel, is where we'll dwell
He'll leave a light on for us, just ring the bell

The twisted heart's knot, He's been untying
As it grows large, you begin to stop crying
Keep hope alive, while dodging those spears
Use your key of life, to lock out the fears

Rock Went a Rollin'

Christ is the controller, of life's video game
With His love in your heart, never be the same
Snowing white butterflies, in summer and winter
Stop feeding your paper, to this dot matrix printer
His love is ablaze, shining so bright
Like Griswold's house, lighting up the night

Lyrics, the colors, in my life of training
My soul's brush is renewed, turn down the complaining
Feel like an artist, in my Father's painting
Blood of the lamb, on my heart it's staining

Easter's the day, the rock went a rollin'
Opened the tomb, that could not hold Him
Christ on the cross, saved us from hell
Holds us together, like a laminin cell
Filling your heart, with our God of creation
Make every day, a Christmas vacation

Holy Spirit powers, gonna activate
In the form of God's love, an open gate
A dynamic duet, singing as one
Jesus lives within you, together we've won
Enjoy this wonderful life, all through the year
Sing His praises, upon a midnight clear

Front row center stage, pony of stone
With Bret Michaels, singing into his microphone
All music moves me, Christ's hand He does extend
To save your soul and live the life, that God did intend

Easter's the day, the rock went a rollin'
Opened the tomb, that could not hold Him
Christ on the cross, saved us from hell
Holds us together, like a laminin cell
Filling your heart, with our God of creation
Make every day, a Christmas vacation

Life's many positive messages, a Nickelback song
About unity and standing strong, we can all get along
Seeing the world as it should be, seems the point has been missed
Awake to see the signs, we'll write a happy ending to this

Remember Christmas and Easter, for their true meaning
No life is too dirty, when God's doin' the cleaning
Jesus Christ's birth, and resurrection
Forever changed, humanity's direction
He died for each of us, once and for all
So we may know him, devil's fire is no match for His call
Don't live too fast, as Clark's siliconed sled
Peaceful feeling of joy, it's in your heart, not your head

Lake Reflection

Time to get things started, time to set things right
Come together now, fight the good fight
God's shining His light, on this world gone astray
Bringing peace that brightens, the darkest of day
Pay attention earth
Here comes the rebirth

Don't just stand and stare
Look to the heavens, and say a prayer
For God is cleaning, up the despair
There are many angels, here day and night
Battling monsters, hidden from sight

Lake reflection, of the albatross that has risen
Found the key in the water, while fishing under the prism
God will take away the sadness
No longer run by the madness
The battle has already been won
Becoming many through one

Hate that dwells, in the shadows of night
Can no longer hide, it's being brought to the light
Jems of knowledge, more radiant than before
Stepping through, a luminous waterfall door

We're all so strong
You know the song
We'll do whatever it takes
As God has upped the stakes
Lessons to be learned, through failure and weakness
A Luke message of strength, in building completeness

Lake reflection, of the albatross that has risen
Found the key in the water, while fishing under the prism
God will take away the sadness
No longer run by the madness
The battle has already been won
Becoming many through one

Isaiah 40:31 (KJV)

"But they that wait upon the Lord shall renew their strength; they shall mount up with wings as eagles; they shall run, and not be weary; and they shall walk, and not faint."

Stars of This Life

Paramedic my label, in the air and the street
Always busy and runnin', many people we meet
Difficult at times, the life of a first responder
In Emergency Services, you know our minds can wander
So many horrors, we can't unsee
From Medical, to Fire, and also PD
Movies in our minds, wish they wouldn't be
Nurses and Doctors, and all hospital staff
To deal with our troubles, we try to joke and laugh

No matter your title, or initials 'round your name
We all have struggles, and deal with different types of pain
We're out there battling, a spiritual syncope of our own
Always caring for others, while our health we postpone
Maintained strength, throughout this career
After many years, surprised to still be here
Tell your family you love them, seen countless lives end too soon
Battled demons within me, not just during the full moon

We're all stars of this life, don't let that light burn out
We've answered a calling, it's what our lives are about
The job takes a toll, for all that respond
No matter the patch, we serve above and beyond

Hours are long, handlin' everyone's issues
Couldn't deal with my own, cryin' fears into tissues
Started to become, Dr. Jekyll and Mr. Hyde
While fighting my thoughts, of who am I inside
I called to Jesus please rescue me, while on my third watch
He responded in an instant, blocked the devil's kick to my crotch

Working days or nights, many years a reaper fighter
We've touched so many lives, and made things brighter
Do not forget those, that answer the phone
Dispatching the units, so no one's alone
Armed forces around the world, responding too
Fighting battles of freedom, for me and for you

We're all stars of this life, don't let that light burn out
We've answered a calling, it's what our lives are about
The job takes a toll, for all that respond
No matter the patch, we serve above and beyond

Ed we miss you, touched our hearts with comedic style
No matter your pain, you always made us smile
George my friend, your pain I hadn't forecast
Then and now, you're the star of the class
A list that is long, of many family and friends
Who've left us too soon, their souls transcend

Told those tales from the dark side, to a new therapist
One that wasn't on, my health insurance list
Jesus my provider, now the only plan I'm with
A new healthy apple, from granny smith
Mending my heart, set my mind at ease
Didn't even realize, I was in a deep freeze

We're all stars of this life, don't let that light burn out
We've answered a calling, it's what our lives are about
The job takes a toll, for all that respond
No matter the patch, we serve above and beyond

Stress on your mind, body, family and friends
During life's struggles, our caring never ends
Brian Regan at the ER, as my valet
Parks my heart with laughter, in a new spot today

No more pills, no more booze
No longer have the blues
Happy thoughts I now ponder
No more nightmares, for this First Responder

Psalms 23:4 (KJV)

"Yea, though I walk through the valley of the shadow of death, I will fear no evil: for thou art with me; thy rod and thy staff they comfort me."

My Father in All

As I laid in bed, looked down the hall
What did I see, my Father in all
Let me explain, just what I saw
It was Jesus, at the end of the hall
Scared and confused, was just a kid
Under the covers, is where I hid

Struggled in life, and now much older
Finally turned around, when You tapped on my shoulder
Excited to know, Jesus is my friend
Standing by Your side, best friends 'til the end

Thank You to, my Father in all
For picking us up, no matter how much we fall
I may not be, very good at math
But the equation I've solved, has led to Your path

Decision plus emotion
That equals devotion
There aren't any problems, only solutions
It has begun, the love revolution

It's now time for us, to live as one
The class we're in, is math 101
No need to worry, God's already won
New morning is dawning, here comes the Son

Thank You to, my Father in all
For picking us up, no matter how much we fall
I may not be, very good at math
But the equation I've solved, has led to Your path

Psalms 28:7 (KJV)

"The Lord is my strength and my shield; my heart trusted in him, and I am helped: therefore my heart greatly rejoiceth; and with my song will I praise him."

53

Brotherly Love

My man Pierre, you know he's on the air
MMR's the station, rockin' all across the nation
Put on your old Victrola
We love that rockin' rolla
Everything that rocks, you know Philly's got soul
Eagles 2018, dramatic fourth down and goal
Training, skill, and prayer, led them to the victory
Philly Special forever, changed the city's history
By the wings of the Eagles, they swept up the champion's bowl
Teamwork and dedication, accomplished that goal

His love is always shining
In our playbook of silver linings
Harry Kalas makes the call
He's got high hopes for us all
While tailgating in this life, there's no misteak on God's grill
City of brotherly love, let's keep spreading good will

Award winning crew, Preston and Steve show
Your love's Philabudance, you help so many we know
We all wanna take, a walk on that stage
Be a baby Jovi, no matter what the age
Will Smith, the Roots in Philly, to sound the horn
Bradley Cooper and Lady Gaga, a star is born
Have a sixth sense, wisdom and knowledge I suppose
In the hall of fame garden, growing a Pete rose
With God's light from above, shines down so bright
It's always sunny in Philadelphia, day or M. Night

His love is always shining
In our playbook of silver linings
Harry Kalas makes the call
He's got high hopes for us all
While tailgating in this life, there's no misteak on God's grill
City of brotherly love, let's keep spreading good will

Rocky Balboa, battling in the ring
God's love it will, take away the sting
Fighting those demons, with fire proof boxing gloves
Bandstand dancing to the music, that everyone loves
A wild heart of Pink, we've joined the rally cry
Fighting for the truth, a soulful freedom butterfly
Practicing banjo strummer, all throughout the summer
For the winter's, Broad street strut of the Mummers
You know we love our Wawa, 24/7 their lights are on
Just a few things, representing in this jawn

His love is always shining
In our playbook of silver linings
Harry Kalas makes the call
He's got high hopes for us all
While tailgating in this life, there's no misteak on God's grill
City of brotherly love, let's keep spreading good will

Here's a little ditty 'bout the crew in this city
From Franklin the Dog to Soul Man and Gritty
We're all Philly Phanatics, stronger as one team
We got Phang in the Union, it's not a pipe dream
No matter your team, Swoop in and have fun
We're all different mascots, that come together as one
Spread that love, raise the city high above
Just my way to show Philly, some brotherly love
You can hear LaBelle a ringing, at Independence Hall
Let's get back to unity, with liberty and justice for all

His love is always shining
In our playbook of silver linings
Harry Kalas makes the call
He's got high hopes for us all
While tailgating in this life, there's no misteak on God's grill
City of brotherly love, let's keep spreading good will

Gateway to God

Many years of sickness, power, money and greed
They took away God's medicine, something that we all need
Cannabis never harmed anyone, yet it's an illegal weed
Slow your life down, take some time to unwind
Avoid negativity, and always be kind
Number 5 is alive, on this Logan's run
Let's all come together, and live as one

Found the golden ticket, that opened the factory gate
Inherited His castle, morals, values and fate
Willie, Wiz and Webby, rollin' violet blueberry
Listening to music makers, while dreamin' of snozberries
Use your imagination, the world we can change
Follow the Lord's path for you, it's been prearranged

Cannabis the gateway, the gateway to God
Weaning you from sickness, to the world you forgot
Zero overdose statistic, with a calming of your mind
The world's herb garden, not surprised to find
The medicine you need, was inside you all the time
Evil's been busy, but it's God's time to shine

Let 'em say we're crazy, we know they're not right
Feelin' at peace, while standing in His light
Like the warmth of sunshine, sweet taste of honey
Enjoy simple things, even without money
So much better, than the pills before
My mind was a prisoner, in someone else's war

Seems for many, good thoughts have declined
Evil had them programmed, to be so blind
Be like Ralphie with Jesus, turning shake into kind
Miss you my friend, you have one funny mind
That ice cream truck is playing, our favorite tune
No matter your flavor, go grab your spoon

Cannabis the gateway, the gateway to God
Weaning you from sickness, to the world you forgot
Zero overdose statistic, with a calming of your mind
The world's herb garden, not surprised to find
The medicine you need, was inside you all the time
Evil's been busy, but it's God's time to shine

Dispensaries helping people, with their cannabis needs
State's tax revenue, funding services with their proceeds
Many delivery methods, to get treatment with CBD oil
A multitude of benefits, from a plant in earth's soil
An opioid solution, you can grow in your home
Don't dismiss it, do some research of your own
Add hemp to your search, many uses it reinforces
Endless possibilities, of nature's abundant resources

Race, color, gender and religious creed
We're all no different than weed
Just varieties in strains
With so many endless names
Try to relax, and stop with the labels
They're breaking our backs, time to turn the tables
The gateway's just the key
Call to Jesus, and you'll see

Had a close encounter, of a Mozart mind
Writing is the gift, that I've been assigned
The path you're on, can go either way
Gotta love one another, who are we to say
We're a rainbow of colors, that equal the same
All are one in this world, start relieving the pain
No need to compare, just be yourself
We're all our own novel, on life's bookshelf

Cannabis the gateway, the gateway to God
Weaning you from sickness, to the world you forgot
Zero overdose statistic, with a calming of your mind
The world's herb garden, not surprised to find
The medicine you need, was inside you all the time
Evil's been busy, but it's God's time to shine

Deceitful propaganda, brainwashed into a sin
Nature's endless healing properties, God's medicine
For every type of illness, from arthritis to cancer
A balance for our body, there is a better answer
The gateway leads to an exit door, from evil's grasp you'll escape
Opens a window to truth, flip side two of life's mixtape

Learn the truth that's out there, before you swallow that pill
Some things you think are helping, are making you ill
Ask the families that are moving, from the state they are in
To cure disease, and stop the seizures of their children
People are no longer sitting idle, as a mute swan
Love tried in the sixties, and now it's back on

From Kottonmouth messages, to a remix from Afroman
Some positive news with Snoop, as your anchorman
We can all be preachers and teachers, it's not wrong
On life's many roads, while rollin' with Cheech and Chong
Sort through the deception, we can all get along
Open your mind to see, the lies that divide us
We're one race of humans, choose the love that's inside us

Genesis 1:12 (KJV)

"And the earth brought forth grass, and herb yielding seed after his kind, and the tree yielding fruit, whose seed was in itself, after his kind: and God saw that it was good."

The Music We All Sing

Twinkle twinkle, a star that's never far
Now I truly know, just who you are
Above this world and in our hearts, He is always standing by
His love shines bright, in a diamond swimming pool sky
We've heard it all before
Life's a Bible metaphor

Swinging a piano hammer, of notes on His music stand
God's peace and love we're sending, all over this land
Perfect harmony, the music we all sing
Come join the band, for together it will bring
Melodic tones are blossoming, God's green thumb
This season of singing, a renewal has begun

Music's in the wind, the trees, and sounds of the night
God is in the rain, washing away the pain and fright
The voice that's been whispering, the doubt and despair
That devil's banished from my mind, with God's Word in prayer
In the deafening sound of silence, and roar of crashing waves
Let everyone remember, as we are spending, Jesus Saves

Swinging a piano hammer, of notes on His music stand
God's peace and love we're sending, all over this land
Perfect harmony, the music we all sing
Come join the band, for together it will bring
Melodic tones are blossoming, God's green thumb
This season of singing, a renewal has begun

Play connect the dots, with the stars in the sky
Draw whatever you like, no need to ask why
His children are looking up, our peace is amplified
Through encouraging words, I will praise You and testify

God's love comes through the voices, like that of a Daigle angel
You say who, I say you, and all that are faithful
Looking down upon us, helping us take a stand
A new temple for the King, He's the leader of our band

Swinging a piano hammer, of notes on His music stand
God's peace and love we're sending, all over this land
Perfect harmony, the music we all sing
Come join the band, for together it will bring
Melodic tones are blossoming, God's green thumb
This season of singing, a renewal has begun

Psalms 100:1-2 (ESV)

"Make a joyful noise unto the Lord, all the earth! Serve the Lord with gladness! Come into his presence with singing!"

Starfighters Unite

There's a universal battle, of this world supernatural
Many so-called truths of history, may not be factual
Wake up to the insanity, the devil's led us astray
Exercise your spiritual muscle, build it stronger everyday
For years I was blinded, by society's myths
Never looking back, it's Jesus I'm ridin' with
When things overwhelm, and you feel you can't cope
Remember to pray, with Him there's always hope

Bringing peace back to our home, folding time beyond
Taking time machine rides with the doctor, 'cross the starry pond
Passed through the black hole, found a rainbow horizon
New beginning at the end, our souls they are arisin'
The star sailors are learning, new ancient ways
Excited for the rebel lion, bringing brighter days

Starfighters unite, portal's aligned and activated
Reach out to Christ, His entryway's illuminated
Mystery's been solved, we've identified chevron seven
The puzzle laid before us, a star gateway to heaven

Heard the tolling of the bell, when it began to ring
Our starship knows the way, staying under His wing
Slideshow memories, of things I had forgotten
Dreaming while awake, of which I'm never stoppin'
Star League recruitment mission, for a good that is greater
Gunstar One blasting off, with our navigator

God's spacesuit of many colors, we're all His astronauts
Headed back with Doc Brown, at 1.21 gigawatts
Returned to now, with a new enlightening
Learned about the power, earth's energy and lightning
From galaxy's above, to Atlantis here below
This ship of fantasies, bringing peace to all we know

Starfighters unite, portal's aligned and activated
Reach out to Christ, His entryway's illuminated
Mystery's been solved, we've identified chevron seven
The puzzle laid before us, a star gateway to heaven

We're gathering info, and securing the team
We know the truth is out there, we're sailing the jet stream
Steve Harvey at the helm, with lasers of inspiration
Galaxy's rejoice, got through the trials and tribulations
Evil's empire has been defeated, closed the gate to death's star
Take your soul on an exploration, find out who you really are

Christ has already paid the price, an interstellar insurance premium
Star knight has returned, falcon's soaring this new millennium
Using powers for good, spreading freedom worldwide
Celebrate the victory, may Jesus' name be glorified
Attacks by the pretender, are no match for the Messiah
Battle's not of flesh but the spirit, a call of Jeremiah
In this Starlite trailer park, every one of us is equal
Sometimes our dreams find us, I'm excited for the sequel

While gazing at the sky
With questions how and why
He spoke a lyric music verse
Created earth, us and the entire universe
Grab your life with both hands,
on this ride of space and time
Remove the limits from your mind,
enjoy our Savior's cosmic rhyme

Jeremiah 1:19 (ESV)
"They will fight against you, but they shall not prevail against you, for I am with you, declares the Lord, to deliver you."

World Series of Life

This game won't be, rained out from the storm
Pure adrenaline's kicking in, put on your uniform
Such an inspirational role model, that's Derek Jeter
We can all learn so much, from a natural leader
Time to play ball, one plus three equals the core
Always top of their game, no matter the score
As we head to the field, and go out through those doors
Tap that sign above, thank the good Lord for making us Yours

Striking out in life happens, you just gotta keep swinging
This game isn't over, praise the Lord with our singing
My heart has a Steiner, cert of authenticity
Signed by Christ, filled with Holy Spirit electricity
George is in the booth, as Bob Shepard calls the names
Heaven's Monument Park, God's roster of forever's game
Bald Vinny's creatures in the bleachers, they've got the roll call
The game of life can be stressful, it's not always a fair ball

God's won this World Series of life, there was never any doubt
Always ahead in the count, you just can't strike Him out
An All-Star team, like you've never seen
Angels at the ballpark, legends in this field of dreams

Tampa in the spring, preparing for that large workload
Many situations we're in, like every Seinfeld episode
We looked for the sign to swing, now safe at His home plate
Waved in from the Lord, and our supportive teammates
Opening day excitement, got those cheers set to max
Peanuts, Hebrew National, and some Crackerjacks
We're all working towards, our own old timer's game
To walk through the gates, of God's great hall of fame

We'll all rise above River Ave, in a sky of tiger lily
Heading to the postseason, an October night that's chilly
Running life's bases, with finesse and style of Willie
Some games you will lose, don't let it get depressing
Waking up to play a new game, one of our many blessings
With love in your heart, you can sail any ball outta the park
Radar reads the speed of light, switch turnin' off the dark

God's won this World Series of life, there was never any doubt
Always ahead in the count, you just can't strike Him out
An All-Star team, like you've never seen
Angels at the ballpark, legends in this field of dreams

There are endless players and support, so many to name
Michael Kay with the play by play, Yes, he takes us out to the ballgame
New York Yankees on the radio, everyone's a fan
Call's the games with commentary, Sterling and Waldman
Working behind the scenes, are the staff and ballpark crew
Steinbrenner family and the fans, always tried and true
Thank you all so much, we appreciate what you do

Ninth inning, game 7, with that closer we all know
It's a win with a cutter, from none other than Mo
Multiple times down many runs, but we came back and overcame
Ol' blue eyes plays us out, at the end of every game

God's won this World Series of life, there was never any doubt
Always ahead in the count, you just can't strike Him out
An All-Star team, like you've never seen
Angels at the ballpark, legends in this field of dreams

When life's pennant race is tough, and you're feeling fatigued
God will send out His love, to the worldwide league
In the end we'll all be standing, together as one team
Don't hide the stuff you're made of, dare to live your dream

The Storm

Halloween 2012, they say a storm is coming
Scene from Noah's ark, with such intense flooding
Couldn't have imagined, what soon we would see
That storm of destruction, was hurricane Sandy
Tide had retreated, seemed good to go
Soon took a drastic turn, little did we know
The island was overtaken, the ocean met the bay
Water all around us, with raging fires across the way
Was this really happening, images of judgement day

When we passed through the waters, He was with us
When we passed through the seas, they did not sweep over us
Sailing our vessel, across the rivers of an infinite sky
Heart's now crying tears of joy, flowing from my mind's eye
He lifts us up to higher ground,
above the depths on a rock platform
He always has His eye on us, which is greater than the storm

Little did we know, this was just the beginning
Appeared this destructive force, was now winning
Raging rivers in every direction, surrounded where we live
Seemed we might not make it,
storms fierce anger would not forgive
Roaring wail as the waters, came crashing through our homes
No more land around us, still protected we were not alone

When we passed through the waters, He was with us
When we passed through the seas, they did not sweep over us
Sailing our vessel, across the rivers of an infinite sky
Heart's now crying tears of joy, flowing from my mind's eye
He lifts us up to higher ground,
above the depths on a rock platform
He always has His eye on us, which is greater than the storm

Neighborhood captains coming together, for the rescue cause
A heart for helping others, they weren't looking for applause
Many brought their boats, whatever they may be
Floating down the streets, that have now become the sea
To take the people in their paths, to higher ground
While the ship of fools, was tossed from the lost to found

Hopped in the boat, at the front door of our home
With our dog and our cat, floating through the seafoam
We always can replace, our Carlin stuff of material
Made it out with our lives, another of God's miracles
Thank you for the care and support,
from around the state and country
Providing shelter and warmth, along with food for the hungry
The rescuers and neighbors, so many volunteers
Outpouring of their love, suppressed the worry and fears
In an emotional time of sadness, you helped dry the tears

When we passed through the waters, He was with us
When we passed through the seas, they did not sweep over us
Sailing our vessel, across the rivers of an infinite sky
Heart's now crying tears of joy, flowing from my mind's eye
He lifts us up to higher ground,
above the depths on a rock platform
He always has His eye on us, which is greater than the storm

Through the flood saw that rainbow, now have total recollection
A call waiting in my dreams, to where I made the connection
At world's end, a time or location could be a sonata form
Everyone pulled together, helping others to stay warm
What looked like the end, was only the beginning
Rebuilding even stronger, no surprise God is always winning
For everyone enduring, your own storm of any name
A call to Jesus in the midst, will guide you through the rain

Psalms 107:28-29 (ESV)

"Then they cried to the Lord in their trouble, and he delivered them from their distress. He made the storm be still, and the waves of the sea were hushed."

Our New Pledge

Blessed are those that pray
Now enjoying life everyday
You only see what you wanna see, happy to hear
Blinders are off, we now see so clear

Don't be distracted, with what you see on TV
More destruction being funneled, into you and in me
Negativity overwhelms us, and stirs us with hate
Does this even seem real, I know this can't be our fate
We'll stick together, like overcooked mac
Shake up this snow dome, we can stop the attack

We pledge allegiance to our Lord
Of this entire vast universe
And to His love for which it stands
One soul as part of Christ
Indivisible with peace and freedom for all

Kick back and relax
Time to bury that ax
Go buy the book, you know the one from the Lord
Follow His lead, throughout this crazy chess board
Life's like furniture in a box, you bought from Ikea
Take your time assembling, following instructions is a good idea

Don't let your heart become, a stuffed vacuum of dirt
Fill it with love, empty out the hurt
Put on a Fluffy smile, of happiness and humor
Got some lyrical advice, from Michael Jr.

We pledge allegiance to our Lord
Of this entire vast universe
And to His love for which it stands
One soul as part of Christ
Indivisible with peace and freedom for all

As I stand on the beach
Nothing's outta God's reach
Waving out to a scrolling sea
Not surprised to see, waves back at me
Be happy and forgiving
This life it is for living

Psalms 69:34 (ESV)

"Let heaven and earth praise him, the seas and everything that moves in them."

A Shining Moment

We're taking away the redrum, from society's mirror
Jack's no longer a dull boy, now seeing much clearer
Midnight, the stars and you, God's the earth's film maker
Not putting the horror in movies, He's always been our caretaker
Once you realize and believe, you'll begin to see
We all have special moments, that set our hearts free
Closed that old door, on evil's room 237
Opened a new door, to the gates of heaven

When the beast is coming after you, darkness behind the mask
Devil on your shoulder, anxiety and fear are his tasks
Don't run away, you'll trip, fall down and let out a scream
Get up now and take a stand, this is your life not just a dream
Look to the angel on your shoulder, help lead you outta Hell
You have a choice don't be afraid, to leave this Overlook Hotel

Hear this song that's being sung, in a voice of Vincent Price
Don't back down from fear's challenge, just some friendly advice
His protection's always with us, although it may not be seen
In the scariest of times, and every shining moment in between
When living in a thriller, and a creature's on your trail
Call to the Lord Almighty, with His word you will prevail

As the dark spirit hovers over, just know you will get through
When that evil's about to take your soul, God will save you
Fight the fear and battle, the monsters in this life
You'll see the power's in you, to make them drop the knife
Remove the darkest shadows, from your memory warehouse
Here we come with Duddits, the devil's flames we will douse

The thing takes shape of anyone, when you're lost in the fog
Watch out for the rabid beast, a raging hellhound dog
It sometimes can be misery, and other times redemption
Through these horrors around me, my heart He has strengthened
While having a cup of coffee, a thought came to my mind
Tired of people being mean and nasty, to each other all the time
The broken glass inside my head, is together and shatterproof
It's now open to the Lord, with a permanent Son roof

Hear this song that's being sung, in a voice of Vincent Price
Don't back down from fear's challenge, just some friendly advice
His protection's always with us, although it may not be seen
In the scariest of times, and every shining moment in between
When living in a thriller, and a creature's on your trail
Call to the Lord almighty, with His word you will prevail

We're no longer in fear, of the alien inside
God's love is within us, there's no reason to hide
Send top hat and his shadow people, away from your mind
Show those demons, access to your soul has been declined
The Lord beamed me up, while I was rappin' with Sevin
Closed the upside-down gate, with the crew and Eleven
There are no more nightmares, on any of our streets
The warriors of dreams have conquered, the series is complete
No matter the evil character, one thing's for sure
Always take a stand, and let God's love endure

Proverbs 3:5-6 (ESV)

"Trust in the Lord with all your heart, and do not lean on your own understanding. In all your ways acknowledge him, and he will make straight your paths."

God's Social Media

Not sure why, this way I feel
Things sometimes, no longer seem real
Evil has made, this world seem absurd
Feel comfort every day, as I read His word
The Bible just makes, more sense to me
Than this current portrayal, shown on TV

When Jesus calls or sends a friend request, will you accept
Will you share His peace, or hit decline and reject
Retweet God's love, it's time to subscribe
You'll receive joy, that's hard to describe

I've been trying my best
My whole life seems a test
Only during the times that I kneel
Can I stand against the evil that's real
No longer having anxiety
From just dinner with family
Don't mind the labels, like crazy or nut
'Cause I know God's with me, feel it in my gut
Things can get rough, don't worry they'll improve
I pay more attention, no longer missing my next move

When Jesus calls or sends a friend request, will you accept
Will you share His peace, or hit decline and reject
Retweet God's love, it's time to subscribe
You'll receive joy, that's hard to describe

Since my path is prewritten, all part of God's plan
He's been here with me, since my life began
When looking for answers, as are most
Use hashtag Bible, within your post
Been through a lot, stayed strong to survive
Flew out that cuckoo's nest, happy to be alive
Thank you for, my life savings account
For God's love, is an eternal amount

When Jesus calls or sends a friend request, will you accept
Will you share His peace, or hit decline and reject
Retweet God's love, it's time to subscribe
You'll receive joy, that's hard to describe

I'll fight the good fight,
Morning, noon and night
If trapped in the darkness, I'll reach out for Your light
Peaceful feeling to know, everything is alright
My heart fills with joy
God's love He'll deploy
One more thing, I no longer keep cryin'
Thank You Lord, love your friend forever, Brian

Psalms 119:105 (KJV)
"Thy word is a lamp unto my feet, and a light unto my path."

Nature is Singing

Trees take a deep breath, lungs of the earth
Keepin' us alive, there's no greater worth
Listen to the birds, in your backyard
You'll hear their lyrics, musical greeting card

Birds and trees, singing their hymns
Squirrel's gather nuts, from the tree limbs
Many past lives, always thinking deja vu
Feelin' free talkin', with Tommy from The Who
Listening to music speaking, when I heard the call
With faith that's strong, it's easy to smell the scents of it all

Nature is singing, divine song and dance
Sing out God's love, a poetic romance
The sound of music, a Narnia mirror
Listening now, and I've never seen clearer
Like the flowers, bloomin' up through the snow
Reaching to the sunshine, for that love they know

Bluebird's the place, in Nashville, Tennessee
With Garth and Trisha, we talked over coffee
Let's be frank, you both pour your hearts out to others
The Queen and the king of Studio G, truly love one another

Stop and smell, those flowers of strawberry pez
Don't listen to doubt, no matter what he says
Listen to nature, God's great composer
Playing a free concert, that brings us all closer
Walking in fields of poppies, you've got to stay awake
New sound of the world, stopping tin foil headaches

Nature is singing, divine song and dance
Sing out God's love, a poetic romance
The sound of music, a Narnia mirror
Listening now, and I've never seen clearer
Like the flowers, bloomin' up through the snow
Reaching to the sunshine, for that love they know

Maestro of the plants, all playing a tune
Garden orchestra, on a sunny afternoon
All the world has rhythm, like that of your heart
A backyard sanctuary, where it's all God's art
Glistening cobwebs, playing harp strings
Woodwinds blowing, a change it brings

Psalms 105:2 (ESV)
"Sing to him, sing praises to him; tell of all his wondrous works!"

A Family Guy's Letter to Seth

Hi Seth, it's alternate universe Brian
You don't know me, but lately been cryin'
Depression, anxiety and PTSD, with sudden fears of dyin'
Been pushin' my way through, God knows I've been tryin'

Even as a paramedic, still not knowing my true purpose
Who's been driving this life, seems only a circus
Syd Barrett, Red Baron, what does this even mean
Start livin' life now, remember we all have a dream

Happy there's a Family Guy, using life as the key
Some don't understand, maybe they just don't see
What seems to be, so obvious to me
Showing reality in cartoons, some pretend it can't be

Good and bad truths, in every episode
Life's clues are out there, you just have to decode
While working through struggles, in this world of Quahog
Learn to break free, from this day of groundhog
Seems always the fun ones, are standing up tall
A new season of laughter, all for one and one for all

Most songs and movies, need a Wayons brother
Yelling there's a message, unlike any other
Was feeling like Meg, for most of my years
The sadness and anger's, no longer grinding my gears
Woke up bright and cheerful, from this life's hangover
Calling on the walkie, now the sentence is over
Feeling better now, heart's filled with love I can't describe
Let's all pour out, our positive vibes

Happy there's a Family Guy, using life as the key
Some don't understand, maybe they just don't see
What seems to be, so obvious to me
Showing reality in cartoons, some pretend it can't be

Took me some time, now I'm starting to learn
In my dream I asked you, do you need an intern
I feel my life is now, beginning Act II
So much together, we can all do
Every show has great writing, from an amazing crew
A future flashback, may I please help too
I'll work my way up, and earn my stay
It feels really good writing, the things I have to say

In the GPS of life, at the fork of left or right
Choose the path of forward, a new direction we'll fight
So happy to know, I can write anywhere
Brightens my life, I'm Christopher walkin' on air
Many more pages to say, not worried 'bout pay
Thank you for listening, and have a nice day

Bucket of Love

Buckethead show, front row TLA
Changed my life, don't know what else to say
Thank you for the gift, you gave me that night
Those colors forever, will be shining so bright

Peering over the hills of eternity
Harmony to save all of humanity
Staring at a Cheshire smile moon
Your soul speaks a universal tune

A Buckethead jam, at Disneyland
Ride the bucket of love, to the promised land
Let your mind ponder
With that childlike wonder
Hundreds of songs, to take you away
His guitar's telling, its own screenplay

A favorite character, shredding guitar licks
Slaying the villains, with the strike of a pick
A blast from his phaser, can do the trick
Savin' the day, one show at a time
Playing a Buckethead nursery rhyme

With Bootsy's world wide funk
To a Michael Jordan dunk
For Mom, and watching the boats with my Dad
Mixed in some titles, from the hundreds he's had

A Buckethead jam, at Disneyland
Ride the bucket of love, to the promised land
Let your mind ponder
With that childlike wonder
Hundreds of songs, to take you away
His guitar's telling, its own screenplay

Look for him, and the redeem team
While enjoying this life, and dancing the dream
A watercolor picture, think you'll like it man
Some love and appreciation, from a Buckethead fan

God's Goodness

God shined His light, on the darkness of the day
His love overcomes, all that was once gray
In His glory forever, and ever we shall stay
We start every morning, with in Jesus name we pray
You know love wins, a real fairytale from childhood
Now goodness is back, where evil once stood

Our past passed away
New world with Jesus, is coming our way
Get yourself together, no more runnin' astray
Future's so bright, and it's here to stay
Open your heart, and quiet your mind
Feel God's goodness, just let it shine

This world is changing, it's easy to see
God's love is strong, it's in you and in me
A shower of light, shines all over this land
We're all coming together, to take our stand
My friend Chris Pratt said it, "God is real"
Truth shall set us free, yeah it's a pretty big deal

Our past passed away
New world with Jesus, is coming our way
Get yourself together, no more runnin' astray
Future's so bright, and it's here to stay
Open your heart, and quiet your mind
Feel God's goodness, just let it shine

The ban has been lifted, the new show must go on
Heard the call that was played, from the trumpeter swan
People get ready, the curtain's been brought down
Keep your head in the heavens, with your feet on the ground

Our past passed away
New world with Jesus, is coming our way
Get yourself together, no more runnin' astray
Future's so bright, and it's here to stay
Open your heart, and quiet your mind
Feel God's goodness, just let it shine

God's rescue mission has begun
Coming together, to serve just one
His love is always near
A new beginning is here

John 3:16 (KJV)
"For God so loved the world, that he gave his only begotten Son, that whosoever believeth in him should not perish, but have everlasting life."

Rhyme for Today

I've so much to say, I was all the labels, a mess
Jesus has saved me, to the world I confess
No longer on a midnight run
Life is now a lot more fun
Lose yourself in His glory
We all have a Spielberg, amazing story
Like a children's book, that's fantastical
Who heard the call, in this world that's musical

In Jesus name we pray
Oh by the way, have a nice day
God's molding us from His clay
I write what He tells me to say
Sounds like an Adam Sandler movie, spreading love today
Tellin' the world about His peace that's real, I just may

Major Tom can hear you, the signal's loud and clear
View from heaven is spectacular, now there's nothing to fear
Live like a Life is Good shirt, on your journey's pathway
Take some time to listen, to this rhyme for today

A weirdo older brother, that you never knew
Prozac nation for me, attention deficit for you
A midweek Webby Wednesday, always droppin' fire
Your lyrics lift us higher, causing others to perspire
Calls them out like it or not, Christian's here to stay
Always on top, speaking truth everyday
Letting 'em know, we're not runnin' away
Corruption's going down, God's tired of the foul play

Eminem, I've been listening for years
You've reached us my friend, you wouldn't believe the tears
You and many others, been calming our fears
We're all soldiers of peace, in God's ballet
Gotta prescription for music, from the doctor that's Dre

Major Tom can hear you, the signal's loud and clear
View from heaven is spectacular, now there's nothing to fear
Live like a Life is Good shirt, on your journey's pathway
Take some time to listen, to this rhyme for today

Show me the way in this grand illusion, some thoughts from Styx
All are one together now, this world we're beginning to fix
In this band of unity, we're one big motley crew
The right path is laid before us, the choice is up to you

Glad World

Awake with my dreams, like Joseph
Nice new places, now I'm focused
Rise and shine, happy faces going somewhere
From horror story nightmare's, to peace with the Lord's prayer
Son is bright, wearing clear view glasses
An ark of love, above the sleeping masses
Meet my friends, they go by new tomorrow
Raised our heads, no longer drowned in sorrow

Feel relieved now, that we're all not mad
Dreams in which I'm flying, are the best I've ever had
We're all here to tell you, this life is what you make it
When people stand for something, see through the counterfeit
No longer scary, but a very glad world

Children playing on the swings, they feel good
Adults should feel the way, that every child would
Anything's possible, in this world of a Disney movie
Let's be preachers and play God's music, He wrote it through me
New expression, on this amazing new day
Filled with passion, found a happy new way
Cupid shoots, His worldwide arrow
Unveiling from the shadows, a new tomorrow

Feel relieved now, that we're all not mad
Dreams in which I'm flying, are the best I've ever had
We're all here to tell you, this life is what you make it
When people stand for something, see through the counterfeit
No longer scary, but a very glad world

I'm thankful for, the tears and fears
They led me to, the smiles and cheers
My mind is filled, with rays of sunshine
No more pills, and now I'm fine
Cured the cyst, that was inside my spine
Thank You Father, for resuscitating me
Brought me back, to a true reality

Feel relieved now, that we're all not mad
Dreams in which I'm flying, are the best I've ever had
We're all here to tell you, this life is what you make it
When people stand for something, see through the counterfeit
No longer scary, but a very glad world

Psalms 98:1 (ESV)

"Oh sing to the Lord a new song, for he has done marvelous things..."

Wind of the Wolf

"M" represents the dark storm, that once was my mind
So many thoughts, had been hard to unwind
At times like the wolf, being misunderstood
Then others red riding, in this neighborhood

My palette's splattered blue, of different gradients
Never ending color sounds, all simultaneous
Snake in the grass, is it friend or foe
Trouble sometimes, is that you just don't know
Now poured out the sadness, that was trapped from within
Words or pointing fingers, can't get under my skin

Wind of the wolf, is my coloring book
Voices of strength, bright blue sky outlook
Had struggled before, while searching for meaning
Bible book of instruction, I am believing
Totem body of one, with different spirits of being
Through the foggy lens, I have a new vision of seeing

Breaking the bottle, no longer holding it in
Stood against fear, won the blue ribbon
Stronger inside, battling storms of darkness
Fighting it now, will succeed regardless
Painting that blue, into a new wave of inspiration
I'll never back down, 'cause I was born to win

Blackbird sings of freedom, to the bats of the night
As the deer sees clearly, in the headlight that's bright
This wolf is howling, the breath of many spirits
Endless notes my heart plays, while in one body's appearance
Traits of goodness in battle, forever I'll strive
Being a work in progress, I will survive

Wind of the wolf, is my coloring book
Voices of strength, bright blue sky outlook
Had struggled before, while searching for meaning
Bible book of instruction, I am believing
Totem body of one, with different spirits of being
Through the foggy lens, I have a new vision of seeing

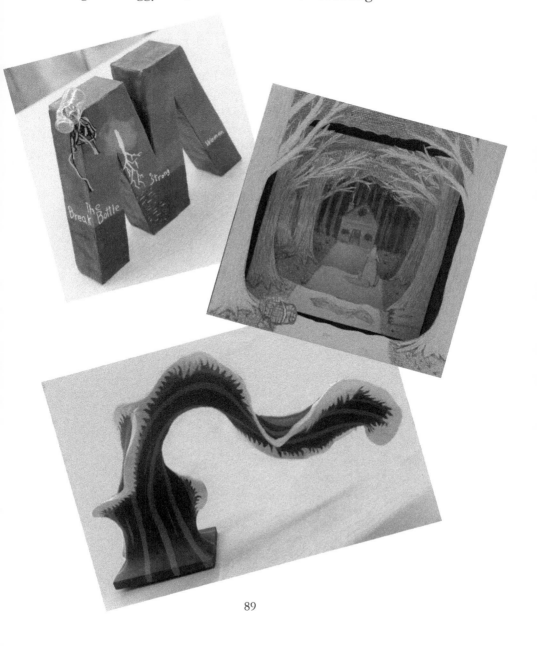

The Gift

Does anyone remember, what Christmas really means
It's in the name and everywhere, so obvious it seems
Climbed that mountain, standing up to see so clear
All of humanity being raised, beyond our atmosphere
When the devil came at me, I showed him some love
He became confused and distraught, so I gave him a hug

Exposing evil while loving, in the world of our Creator
He's the year-round, Christmas party coordinator
Don't let hate overtake, stop feeding the disease
You'll just end up covering, a black eye with frozen peas
Don't let the devil, be your editor or illustrator
For the Word that God has written, is forever greater

Power of prayer will open doors, to that house up on a hill
He's got the key for your new home, this is not a drill
The world's becoming peaceful, Holy Spirit is the gift
Let go of hate and anger, your soul the Lord will lift
Heaven's windows are open, you can hear those angels singing
On a sled of freedom, peace and love we are bringing

Shake hands with the beast, and invite him to the feast
A cold and tiny heart, with love it will increase
Sometimes things are tough, but God gives us strength
Tune into His Christmas carols, feel your heart's wavelength

Hear the joyful singing, bringing unity throughout
He's the reason for the season, for me there is no doubt
In this life you follow, His entire Word that's true
Not just the certain parts, you think will work for you
You'll see the Holy Spirit, who's always been inside
He's the one taking you, on this wondrous ride

Power of prayer will open doors, to that house up on a hill
He's got the key for your new home, this is not a drill
The world's becoming peaceful, Holy Spirit is the gift
Let go of hate and anger, your soul the Lord will lift
Heaven's windows are open, you can hear those angels singing
On a sled of freedom, peace and love we are bringing

Did you ever stop to ask
'Bout the presents throughout this task
His presence is our present
Of which it's time to be present
Think about that, just an example for some
A trio of omni presence, that all equal one
The world is full of different solutions
Choose to be positive, stop the hate pollution

Clean Soul

When you happen to step, in an evil load
While your takin' a walk, down life's winding road
Not to worry, washes right off with a soul that's clean
Just stay positive, you all know what I mean

Wipe your feet, on God's welcome mat
Within His love, is where it's at
There's no load too large
When a clean soul's in charge
God loves us all, not a question of maybe
Love that's the power, of a fine soul baby

No need to worry
Or be in too much of a hurry
Life's meant for livin'
Enjoy what you've been given
Heart's no longer frozen you see
It's now warm, no matter the weather for me

Wipe your feet, on God's welcome mat
Within His love, is where it's at
There's no load too large
When a clean soul's in charge
God loves us all, not a question of maybe
Love that's the power, of a fine soul baby

Just because you smelt it
Doesn't always mean you dealt it
Could be on someone else's shoe
Trying to cling onto you
We can all walk over, the waters of doubt
There's nothing that God, can't wash out
Use a new cleaning solution, one that's easy to obtain
Call on the Lord, for a cleansing shower in His rain

Wipe your feet, on God's welcome mat
Within His love, is where it's at
There's no load too large
When a clean soul's in charge
God loves us all, not a question of maybe
Love that's the power, of a fine soul baby

Psalms 51:10,12 (ESV)

"Create in me a clean heart, O God, and renew a right spirit within me. Cast me not away from your presence, and take not your Holy Spirit from me. Restore to me the joy of your salvation, and uphold me with a willing spirit."

The Answer

Within this book of many rhymes
Stabilized the chronosphere of time
I've a story that never ends
About this society that's all pretend
Upon this desert of shattered hopes
In this swamp of sadness, we'll fight the hoax

Spoke with Melanie, my friend mad hatter
We've much in common, sharing our gray matter
We see things differently than others
While listening quietly to colors
Hymns of angelic harmony, at Alice's restaurant of healing
A groovy movement of peace, with love showing feeling
Expose the secrets, of this wonderland
Against the fallen angels, we take our stand

The grandfather clock, has been rewound
The puzzle's answer, has been found
In this disturbed, land of confusion
Curtain's been lifted, on the snare of illusion
You have a choice, pill of red or blue
Choose the truth, when the caterpillar calls to you
Go ask Alice, who's world's insane
We've found the balance, opened eyes back to sane

God's angel army is everywhere, rider on a white horse
We don't have to hide anymore, love has set the course
Awake and dreaming, breaking through the elsewhere we'll go
Heard that bell ringing, we're going on with God's new show
While sitting in the backyard, conversing with Ronnie
A rainbow in the dark, appeared brightly over me
Feel like Bart from Mercy Me, took a lifetime for this quest
Hopes and dreams are what we need, to live this life so blessed

The grandfather clock, has been rewound
The puzzle's answer, has been found
In this disturbed, land of confusion
Curtain's been lifted, on the snare of illusion
You have a choice, pill of red or blue
Choose the truth, when the caterpillar calls to you
Go ask Alice, who's world's insane
We've found the balance, opened eyes back to sane

A Tim Burton mind, of wondrous imagination
Endless sea of possibilities, an Iron Maiden revelation
With Christ in our hearts, we can always overcome
We are never alone, multiple warriors of one
There are no boundaries for Fantasia, we will do what we dream
He'll lift us up like Falkor, can you picture that scene

Listen for His music, overture of love that's unified
With teardrops of joy, this highwayman's reached the other side
Kaleidoscope eyes, on life's movie screen projecting
A paradise lost, returning soon our soul's reflecting
God's The Answer for us all, what were you expecting

Thank You Song

Hope you have enjoyed, this 3am songbook
A glimpse into my heart, for you all to take a look
In my darkest of nights, the battle had been won
When I called out Your name, together becoming one
Thank You Jesus, my Lord and Savior wearing the crown
My life is just beginning,
now I'm picking up what you're putting down

Where I was only one before, now we are two
You've been helping me since my life began,
I hadn't realized it was You
I've more subject matter to move around,
as I begin this calling of a writer
Wearing sunglasses I'll keep movin' on,
future's never been brighter
Even when I didn't think, I'd get through another day
I've learned to live for You Lord, and follow in Your way

Thank you to my wife Kathie,
here in the good times and sadness
Helping me throughout, the nightmares and the madness
Thank you to our Mom's and Dad's, for never giving up on me
While my heart became a stone, and my soul an absentee
Thank you to all of our family and friends
Many prayed for me, when I was close to the end

Thank you to our family of pets, Sunshine dog of therapy
Without the help from all of them, I don't know where I'd be
Thank you to all at Milestone Church, and to Pastor Bill
My heart that was empty, you have helped refill
Thank you to our tri-state bible study, always on God's radar
I appreciate everyone mentioned, just for being who you are

Thank you to Tonya, you helped me find my pen
Made a difference in my life, God Bless and Amen
Thank you to my coworkers, serving within this vaulted ceiling
An endless list of many others, helping with the healing

Thank you to the songwriters, musicians, writers and singers
Movie makers, entertainers, youtuber's and sports figures
All got me through life's puzzle, your love helped stop my cryin'
This entire book's a thank you note, from this life of Brian

On this new adventure, I've been working overtime
Sorting through the words to write, that are spinning in my mind
Another dream's to hear these lyrics, played on the radio
My heart hears music notes, as works of Michelangelo
I appreciate you the readers, for checking out this book
I pray it has touched you, now that you've taken a look

As this story ends, may I remind you all
Always get back up, when you stumble and fall
Break the doubt that's racked up, cause you're the cue ball
Go live your dream don't hesitate, when you get the call
Always be kind and loving, a heart filled with joy and laughter
Keep God above all things, in life you'll live happily ever after

Thank You!!

Psalms 100:4 (KJV)

"Enter into his gates with thanksgiving, and into his courts with praise: be thankful unto him and bless his name."